Scots Gaelic

an introduction to the basics

George McLennan

ARGYLL✣PUBLISHING
Glendaruel Argyll Scotland

© George McLennan

First published 1987
Gairm Publications, Glasgow

New edition 1998
Argyll Publishing

This edition 2005, reprinted 2010
Argyll Publishing
Glendaruel
Argyll PA22 3AE
www.argyllpublishing.com

Chuidich Comhairle nan Leabhraichean
am foillsichear le cosgaisean an leabhair seo.

British Library Cataloguing-in-Publication Data.
A catalogue record for this book is available from
the British Library.

ISBN 1 902831 88 8

Printing Bell & Bain Ltd, Glasgow

CONTENTS

The need for another reprint of *Scots Gaelic – an introduction to the basics* has enabled me to add further illustrations – for instance, similarities with other European languages – as well as some new material to the book, and to make a few minor changes. I hope that these additions will add to the interest of the book.

Since I constantly hear and read remarks to the effect that Gaelic words are not sounded as they are spelled, I have continued to emphasise the logic and consistency behind Gaelic spelling. Such remarks are quite meaningless since they are always made from the speaker's standpoint, usually the English language and its spelling 'rules'. By such a criterion **any** foreign language is not sounded as it is spelled; no doubt there are many native French speakers who assert that all English words are not sounded as they are spelled!

A discussion I had with a German a few years ago led me to reconsider the title of this book. She was under the impression that Scots meant the Gaelic language, simply because she found that written Scots was so different from English; she was quite fluent in English but could make little of Scots, and knew no Gaelic, although she certainly knew of its existence. So this is perhaps the place to point out to non-Scottish readers that Scots, currently at its strongest in the north east, is a dialect of English, having evolved from earlier Northern Middle English (more Angle than Saxon), whereas modern standard English has evolved from earlier Midland

and Southeastern English (more Saxon than Angle). Gaelic, on the other hand, is a Celtic language, something quite different. Calling this book 'Scottish Gaelic' might possibly have made things clearer, but after some deliberation I have left the title unchanged in the interests of consistency. For the same reason I have retained the *sd* spelling in words such as **pòsda, furasda**, etc, while acknowledging that the latest edition of *Gaelic Orthographic Conventions* recommends replacing *sd* with *st*.

At the end of each chapter, except chapter 9 which deals with place-names in a more structured way, I have added a few place-names derived from words mentioned in that chapter, with a rough guide to their locations. Most of the places have deliberately been chosen from parts of the country where Gaelic has now more or less vanished. This provides evidence, if such were needed, of the wide spread of the language in earlier centuries.

George McLennan
Blairmore, Argyll
September 2005

Preface to the Second Edition

The continuing expansion of interest in Gaelic has led to a demand for a new edition of *Scots Gaelic – a brief introduction*. I have therefore taken this opportunity to expand some of the points made earlier and to give additional illustrations, all of which I hope will make the book more useful.

Now that the potential benefits of bilingualism are fully understood, it is clear that a knowledge of Gaelic as well as English – and/or any other language(s) – is a considerable asset, not, as was sometimes thought, a drawback. In addition, continuing European integration should encourage us to view Gaelic in a European dimension, beyond the traditional Celtic fringe.

Preface to the First Edition

Until quite recently the study of Gaelic has been greatly neglected, even discouraged, in this country. Many Scots who are familiar with other European languages often know little or nothing about Gaelic, and seem to regard it as being somehow outwith the mainstream of European languages.

The purpose of this booklet, then, is to provide a brief introduction to the Gaelic language with a selective discussion of its main features. I have tried to keep things as simple as possible to accommodate readers who may be taking a first look at the language, but those whose knowledge of Gaelic is a little more advanced may also find the booklet useful. Accordingly, while a lot more could be said on many points, and qualifications added here and there, I have preferred to be brief rather than punctilious. Thus, guides to pronunciation, for instance, are inevitably only approximate. Readers should also be aware that Gaelic orthography is not as uniform as that of English, although steps continue to be taken towards an agreed standard. For example, the new system of accentuation (using mainly the grave accent) is used, but a note in chapter 5 describes the older system, in use until very recently in printed books.

In contrast to native speakers, who absorb the language as children, adults who are learning Gaelic from scratch often derive much benefit from knowing **why** the language takes shape as it does. I have tried to bear this in mind throughout the booklet.

S COTS GAELIC belongs to the Celtic branch of the Indo-European family of languages. The other Celtic languages are Irish and Manx (Isle of Man) which, with Gaelic, have a common ancestor called Gadelic; and Welsh, Breton (Brittany, France) and Cornish, whose common ancestor is Brittonic. Today Gaelic, Irish, Welsh and Breton (and, just, Manx) survive as modern examples of the Celtic language which was spoken in many parts of Western Europe – as far east as the Danube – up to the time of the Roman Empire. It was the Romans who destroyed the Celtic languages in mainland Europe, and in their place we find today the Romance languages (Italian, French, Spanish, Portuguese, Romanian etc.), all derived from Latin. Thus the Breton language in France is not indigenous, but was taken there by settlers from Cornwall and Wales around the 5th century AD. Scots Gaelic itself came from Ireland at about the same time, and for many centuries Gaelic and Irish were very similar, at least on a literary level (small though this was).

The point about the Indo-European family of languages, of which Celtic is one branch, is that most of the European languages of today (over 30 of them) go back to a common ancestor called Indo-European. Consequently, we can expect many Gaelic words to be related to, or cognate with, words in other European languages. On a more local level, Gaelic vocabulary obviously has many similarities with Irish, Welsh, etc.; but many learners of Gaelic may be unfamiliar with these languages, and so throughout this booklet a selection of Gaelic words is given with cognates in English.[1]

There are, of course, a large number of words in Gaelic which are simply taken from English, sometimes altered a little and spelt in the Gaelic way: e.g. **botal** for 'bottle', **banca** for 'bank' and so on. As a general rule they represent things outside the traditional Gaelic environment, such as words for 'factory', 'hospital' etc. and the machines found in them. This is especially true of modern scientific terms – television, car, rocket etc. In many cases Gaelic words have in fact been created for such words – **x-ghath** for 'x-ray', for instance – but most native speakers use the English word. Often they would not be familiar with the newly created Gaelic word, so that if one hears e.g. **saideal** for 'satellite' on the radio, it is usually accompanied by an English 'translation' – at least the first time round – to make it understood. However, efforts in Gaelic broadcasting to strive towards a Gaelic unadulterated by constant intrusions of English are a welcome sign.

This use of English words has, of course, the advantage of making Gaelic easier for a learner to understand, even if the words are in Gaelic dress, e.g. **depeandadh** for 'depending', or **smocadh** for 'smoking'. In addition to the many English words in Gaelic there are many from Scots, often reflecting Scots pronunciation, e.g. **gròiseid**, 'grosset' (gooseberry), or **saighdear**, 'soldier'.

However, the vast majority of Gaelic words are, of course, not borrowed from English, though many have cognates with English. Thus **eaglais**, 'church', needs only a moment's

---

1. Sometimes, of course, a cognate is more clearly seen in another European language; e.g. **muileann** (mill) and French *moulin*, **caraid** (friend) and Italian *caro*, **fhuair** (found) and Greek (Archimedes) *heureka*.

thought before one sees the connection with 'ecclesiastic'. Since it is much easier to learn vocabulary if one can see such connections, a list of words will be given at the end of each chapter, with cognates in English. It is often a question of not seeing the wood for the trees. English is unusual in that it is a language composed of two separate strata – 1) a Germanic one, the basis, and 2) a classical (mainly Latin) one. The latter is a more learned, artificial stratum. It is as if there were two languages within English, either one capable of being translated into the other. Thus 'two-yearly' (Germanic) = 'biennial' (Classical), 'cogitate' (Classical) = 'think' (Germanic) and so on.

Generally, of course, good written English combines the two strata although it is often possible to write predominantly in one as opposed to the other. Many Gaelic words, then, are cognate with the learned, classical word in English, as in the case of **eaglais**. Equally, many Gaelic words are cognate with an English word which is slightly removed in meaning from the immediate English translation, although the connection is usually clear enough. Here are some examples:

VOCABULARY

GAELIC	ENGLISH	ENGLISH COGNATE
aifreann	mass (religious)	offering
bàirneach	limpet	barnacle
cailc	chalk	calcium
dall	blind	dull
each	horse	*eq*uine
facal	word	vocal
gailleann	storm	gale

[handwritten margin note: barnyach, kalk]

ifrinn	hell	infernal
leabhar	book	library
madainn	morning	matins
nathair	snake	adder (orig. nadder)
obair	work	*ope*rate
peileir	bullet	pellet
rannsaich	search	ransack
sagart	priest	*sacerd*otal, sacred
tana	thin, shallow	*ten*uous
uileann	elbow	ulna

Some place names derived from words mentioned in this chapter.

Eaglais – Church
Eaglesham (Renfrewshire)
Gleneagles (Perthshire)

Muileann – Mill
Lagavullin (Islay)
Milngavie (Dumbartonshire)

Each – Horse
Loch Eck (Argyll)

Tana – Thin, Shallow
the Tan (water between the Cumbraes, Ayrshire)

CHAPTER 2
LENITION/ASPIRATION

LENITION, formerly (and less correctly) called aspiration, is one of the chief difficulties for learners of Gaelic. On paper it takes the form of a letter 'h' inserted after a consonant and is very frequent in Gaelic (and even more frequent in pseudo-Gaelic). Lenition is the lightening or softening of a consonant when it occurs between two vowels. In going from one vowel to the other the consonant in between is not made in the normal way, but extra air is allowed through. For instance, the clear, crisp sound of 'c' (as in English 'cut') becomes, when lenited, 'ch' (as in 'loch'). In other words, the tongue in this case does not go all the way through with its usual movement towards the roof of the mouth to produce 'c' but stops short, and 'ch' results.

In a sense it is a kind of relaxation of pronunciation in that the effort is not made to make the clear consonant sound between vowels, and so the lightened, or lenited consonant results. This does not mean, of course, that there is anything slovenly about it. Every language has its own ways of adapting sounds in various uses and combinations to suit the speakers of that language.

Thus in the English of southern England a final 'r' is not pronounced, nor, colloquially, is an initial 'h'. The famous Scots glottal stop, where the 't' in, e.g. 'water' is lightened in sound so as to almost disappear, has a resemblance to the lightened consonant in Gaelic. Modern French also provides numerous examples, as *croire* (to believe) from Latin *credere* (whereas Italian *credere* keeps the 'd'). Gaelic lenition, of course, is a well established, and in the correct circumstances, which will be explained later, a quite obligatory feature of the language.

The difficulty for beginners is the different sounds some of the consonants make when lenited. Here are the lenited Gaelic consonants with the phonetic English equivalents:

bh = v

ch = ch

dh = gh (with a broad vowel) or y (with a slender vowel). See chapter 3

fh is silent

gh = gh or y, as with dh above

mh = v

ph = f

sh = h

th = h

It may be hard for beginners in the language to see why 'bh', for instance, should have the sound of 'v'. In fact the 'h' is only a symbol indicating that the consonant is lenited; at one time a dot above the letter did the same job. The sounds of 'ch' (as in 'loch') and 'ph' (as in 'photograph') are more obvious, but in any case 'h' is the traditional letter in European languages used, when placed after a consonant, to indicate that the consonant has changed its sound in some way.

In English, of course, 'ch', 'ph', 'sh', 'th', and 'wh' have a different sound from the same letters without the added 'h', and 'gh' also indicates a hard 'g' as in 'gherkin'. In Italian too it is used to change the sound of 'g' with a slender vowel ('e' and 'i') from soft to hard, so that *spaghetti* is sounded with the 'g' hard; without the accompanying 'h' it would be soft, like the 'g' in *Genoa*. It also changes the sound of 'c', so that in *Chianti*, the 'h' makes the 'c' hard (like 'k'); without the 'h' before a slender vowel it would be soft, as in *cello*. Portuguese, again, uses 'h' to alter the sound of the consonants 'l' and 'n', giving 'nh' a *ny* sound like the sound in the middle of the English word 'onion', so that Portuguese *senhor* is Spanish *señor* (Mr., Sir), *canhao* is *cañon* (canyon) etc. **So the letter 'h' is a prime candidate for indicating changes to the sounds of consonants.**

Many of the lenited Gaelic consonants have interesting parallels in Europe. A modern Greek and Russian b is pronounced 'v', and both letters have a similar sound in Spanish; in the Germanic language family 'b' and 'v' are often interchangeable, hence English 'have' but German *haben*. The same variation is found in Spanish and Portuguese. Lenited 'm' also has this 'v' sound, as can be seen above. There is, of course, a similarity between 'm' and 'b', in that they are both voiced bilabials. A 'b' is often not sounded after an 'm' when they occur together; because of their similarity only the first consonant need be sounded. This is known as eclipsis; an example in Gaelic would be **tìr nam beann,** 'land of the mountains', where the 'b' is often not sounded, or the village of Munlochy, **Bun Lòchaidh** in Gaelic. An example in English would be 'numbskull'.

A modern Greek gamma ('g') followed by a slender vowel is pronounced 'y'(as in 'yet'), and, to take an illustration closer to home, *yett* is a Scots variant of 'gate' (hence the surnames Yates/Yeats). With regard to the silent 'fh' of Gaelic, Spanish often does not sound an initial 'f' from Latin (e.g. *hado* – 'fate' – Latin *fatum*, Italian *fato*, etc). In such cases the 'h' is not sounded in modern Spanish, but it was in the sixteenth century, when the initial sound resembled that of the Gaelic words **fhathast** 'still', 'yet', **fhein** 'self' and **fhuair** 'found', 'got', which, exceptionally, have an initial 'h' sound. And 'p' and 'f' are often interchangeable within the Germanic languages, e.g. 'ship' and German *Schiff.*

Even the English language can, indirectly, illustrate this phenomenon; lenited 's' with its resulting 'h' sound has parallels in Greek (which uses the letter 'h' where Latin has 's') and Latin (which uses the letter 's' where Greek has 'h'). Hence English, with its customary widespread borrowing from the classical languages has '**h**exagon' (from Greek) and '**s**extet' (from Latin), both based on the meaning 'six', '**h**eptagon' and '**s**eptet', both based on the meaning 'seven', '**h**emisphere' and '**s**emicircle', both meaning 'half' and so on. **So the point to bear in mind in all this is that these different sound shifts in Gaelic lenition/aspiration are in no way arbitrary, but rather reflect traditional Indo-European sound changes.**

It is when listening to spoken Gaelic that learners find lenition difficult. A word which begins with, say, 'b' will sometimes begin with the sound 'v' – and so on with the other consonants. So, most words beginning with consonants have two ways of being pronounced initially, depending on the grammatical circumstances. One has to learn two words, as it were. Thus the Gaelic for 'cow' is **bò** (unlenited) or **bhò** (lenited) and the sounds are 'bo' and 'vo' respectively.

This feature is found in other European languages, and even in some African languages, but it is above all a phenomenon of the Celtic languages. Scots Gaelic is particularly fond of it, more so than its parent Irish. It has often been remarked that some languages, e.g. Latin and its modern derivatives, have *endings*, whereas the Celtic languages have *beginnings*. This is certainly true, but is not the whole story; Celtic languages too have *endings*, and even '*middlings*', which can make things harder for learners!

Beginners, noting that both 't' and 's' when lenited have the same sound (h), as do 'b' and 'm' (v), may wonder if this causes difficulties in spoken Gaelic. In theory uncertainty is possible; **shèid**, 'blew' and **thèid**, 'will go', sound much the same, as do the lenited forms **bhaoth**, 'simple', 'silly' and **mhaoth**, 'soft', 'tender'. But the context, and the judicious use of synonyms if necessary, always makes the meaning clear.

When consonants are lenited in the middle, or at the end, of words they are frequently not sounded at all. Thus **deigh**, 'ice' is pronounced 'jayi'. This is easier to understand as it frequently happens in English, e.g. 'high', 'sigh', 'throughout'. At an earlier stage in the language such consonants were pronounced, both in Gaelic (**Gài**_dh_**lig** > Gadelic) and in English, which is why they still appear in the word, though now silent. They may, in fact, still be sounded in a cognate in another language; for instance the 'g' is pronounced in German _burg_ ('town', Hamburg, Salzburg, etc) but in Scots _burgh_ the hard 'g' sound has gone. A silent lenited/aspirated consonant in English is often sounded elsewhere in Europe – thus Scots and German _licht_, but English 'light'.

Lenition **inside** a word takes place when an **original single** consonant which lends itself to lenition is found between two vowels. The reason for the lenition in, say, **slighe** ('path', 'way') but not in **slige** ('a shell') is because the latter type illustrates the following point : the single 'g' of **slige**, _as it is spelled today_, represents an earlier stronger sound, two consonants, perhaps a double 'g', and this was too 'heavy' to be affected by lenition. **Slighe** on the other hand had only the single consonant – 'g' in this case – sound, and so became a candidate for lenition. Final consonants are also lenited or unlenited for the same reason.

Gaelic has gradually been increasing the use of lenited consonants over the centuries, and, as befits a living language, the process continues today. For instance **dhomh**, 'to me', is now far commoner than the rarely heard initially unlenited form **domh**. Sometimes, too, a final consonant may, or may not, be lenited, depending on the speaker. Thus the adverb **gu h-àraid**, 'especially', is given a final 'j' sound by some speakers, but there is also a lenited form **gu h-àraidh**, where the final 'dh' is not sounded at all.

Gaelic has at least retained such lenited consonants in its spelling, even if they are not pronounced, and this can make a word easier to understand. Thus **màthair**, 'mother' is pronounced 'ma-h-er', but because the 't' is written we can see the obvious connection with 'maternal' etc. French *mère*, in contrast, also cognate with Latin *mater*, has typically lost the 't' from both sound and spelling.

Sometimes a lenited consonant inside a word may, or may not, be sounded, depending on the speaker. For instance **àbhaist**, 'usual', is often heard with the 'v' sound in the middle, but many speakers leave it out.

Initial Lenition
There are, of course, grammatical rules which dictate when the first consonant of a word must be lenited and they are found in all grammars. Briefly, the main occasions are:

a) Verbs – to form the past tense e.g. **cùm**, 'keep', **chùm e**, 'he kept'.

If the verb begins with a vowel or 'f' then it cannot be lenited in the normal way; instead, 'dh' is put in front of it. This 'dh' is connected with the particle **do** which was a sign of the past tense, still found in negatives and questions. Thus **dh'òl mi**, 'I drank', **dh'fhàg mi,** 'I left'.

Another tense which is lenited is the subjunctive (= would) e.g. **chanainn**, 'I would say'.

b) Nouns, if they are feminine, are lenited after the definite article singular e.g. **muir**, 'sea', **a' mhuir**, 'the sea'.[1]

After a preposition with the definite article both masculine and feminine nouns are lenited (although not all consonants do it) e.g. **air a' bhòrd**, 'on the table'.

c) Adjectives, which in Gaelic usually follow the noun, are lenited if the noun is feminine e.g. **tè bheag**, 'a small one', 'a dram'.

d) A very few adjectives precede their noun, and in this case the noun is lenited. The most common adjectives to do this are **droch**, 'bad', **deagh**, 'good', and **ath**, 'next'. Some other words cause lenition in nouns or adjectives which follow them, most notably **mo**, 'my', **do**, 'your', **a**, 'his' and **glè**, 'very'.

References above to masculine and feminine nouns indicate a major difference from English, where nouns are neutral. Gaelic has masculine and feminine nouns, and used to have a third, neuter, type, as German, for instance still has. Learners may wonder if there is any indication contained in the word itself as to its gender. There are some: the diminutive ending **-an** indicates a masculine noun, as in **lochan**, 'a small loch'; the diminutive ending **-ag** is feminine, so **duilleag**,

---

1. The reason for this is that in Gadelic the feminine singular definite article ended in a vowel (as is normal in European languages) and so the first consonant of the following noun is flanked by two vowels and is therefore lenited. The masculine definite article ended in a consonant and so there is no lenition. In the genitive singular, on the other hand, the masculine article did end in a vowel, which is why masculine nouns with the article are lenited in the genitive singular.

'leaf', is feminine. And words ending in **-air** indicating a trade or activity are masculine, as **clachair**, 'mason'.

Beyond this there are guidelines, but exceptions abound. The ending **-ag**, for instance, mentioned above, may be neither a diminutive nor feminine. **Aiseag**, 'a ferry', a very common word on Highlands and Islands timetables, is usually masculine (hence Ardanaseig – Ferry Point – on Loch Awe, Argyll). Nor is the meaning of a word a reliable guide; **boireannach**, 'woman' is masculine; and **feusag**, 'beard' is feminine, which might seem inappropriate, but, of course, it is an example of the feminine diminutive **-ag** mentioned above. Nor can the gender of a cognate always help – **abhainn**, 'river' is feminine, but the related Latin *amnis* is generally masculine. Even directly-borrowed words are unreliable: **achd**, 'an act' is feminine but the Latin word from which it is borrowed – *actum* – is neuter. Analogy is a likely explanation for much of this. Nouns borrowed into Gaelic would have a strong tendency to take the gender of the majority of existing Gaelic words with an ending similar to the newly borrowed word. It should be noted, also, that many nouns can be masculine in one district yet feminine in another. **Aiseag,** 'a ferry', for instance, mentioned above as being usually masculine, can be feminine in some areas, hence **Rubha na h-Aiseig** in Trotternish, Skye.

It was mentioned at the beginning of this chapter that aspiration was a conventional, if unsatisfactory, term for the process subsequently discussed. True aspiration (aka preaspiration), however (i.e. the insertion of the *sound* 'h'), is a feature of Gaelic and is frequently found in short syllables before 'c', 'p' and 't'. Thus **cat**, 'cat' is pronounced 'caht', **mac**, 'son' is pronounced 'mahc', and so on. This was a linguistic feature of the old Norse of the Vikings and is a legacy of their stay in the Highlands and Islands.

VOCABULARY

GAELIC	ENGLISH	ENGLISH COGNATE
ainm	name	*onom*atopoeia, an*onym*ous
bata	stick	bat
Callainn	New Year's Day	calendar
diathad, dìot	dinner	diet
eadar	between	*inter*national
fear	man	*vir*ile
geòla	small boat	yawl
luach	value, worth	lucre
maide	stick	mast
a-nochd	tonight	*noct*urnal
òraid	speech	oration
pàisd	child (esp.male)	page
rìgh	king	*reg*al
saighead	arrow	*Sagitt*arius
tìr	land	*terr*ain

Some place names derived from words mentioned in this chapter.

Bò – Cow
Bealach nam Bò (Ross and Cromarty; Perthshire)

Màthair – Mother
Motherwell

Muir – Sea
Achnamara (Argyll)

Beag – Small
Larachbeg (Morvern)
Drumbeg (Sutherland)

21

Cat – Cat
Ardchattan (Argyll)

Mac – Son
Balmaclellan (Dumfries and Galloway)
Balmacara (Ross and Cromarty)

Slige – Shell
Pitsligo (Aberdeenshire)
Sligachan (Skye)

Tìr – Land
Tiree (Argyll)
Chirmorie (Ayrshire)
Auchtertyre (Angus; Ross and Cromarty)

Abhainn – River
Portnahaven (Islay)
Garrynahine (Lewis)

CHAPTER 3
SPELLING

GAELIC SPELLING follows clear rules, and is no better or no worse than English in this respect once the rules are understood, and, as a bonus, the sounds produced within the spelling system are a lot more consistent than those of English.

George Bernard Shaw's well-known remark that the word 'fish' could well be spelled 'ghoti' (gh=f as in 'rough'; o=i as in 'women'; ti=sh as in 'nation') is an amusing illustration of the spelling peculiarities of English. Consider also that the sound ee (as in 'feet') can be written at least a dozen different ways in English, viz. e (he), i (mi – sol-fa), ee (see), ea (sea), ey (key), ay (quay), ie (yield), ei (receipt), eo (people), ae (caesarean), i-e, (marine), e-e, (here). Gaelic by contrast, just uses the letter 'i', with an accent to indicate a long sound; so **fir**, 'men', **cìr**, 'a comb'. Sometimes it may have the letter 'o' next to it to indicate the sound of the following consonant, with the 'o' not sounded, as explained below; so **fios**, 'knowledge' – without the 'o' the 's' would have been pronounced like English 'sh'.

But learners of the language, faced with a long Gaelic word half the letters of which do not seem to be pronounced, often do not know where to start! Even native speakers, particular of the older generation, can often be in difficulties, for several reasons. Firstly, the shameful attitude of education authorities in the past to Gaelic meant that Gaelic speaking children were, to a large extent, denied an opportunity to be fully literate in their language. Fortunately this attitude has changed greatly in recent years and present trends are very encouraging. Secondly, there has been, until relatively recently, a dearth of reading material in Gaelic, particularly of newspapers and other lighter material. Gaelic books in the past tended to be of a serious, often religious nature, with little suitable for children, for instance. Again, encouraging steps have been taken in recent years to remedy this. Above all, of course, Gaelic has for some centuries been part of an oral culture in which literacy was not essential, and written English was always used when required.

The main feature of Gaelic spelling is the use and influence of the vowels. These are divided into two groups.

a) A O U, the broad vowels,

and b) E I, the narrow or slender vowels.[1]

Such a division is, of course, common in other European languages, and, as in Gaelic, has an effect on the sound of a consonant next to the vowels. In English, for instance, the letter 'c' is pronounced hard (k) with a broad vowel (cat, cot, cut) but soft (s) with a slender vowel (cell, city). This is fairly widespread; compare, e.g. Italian *Caruso* and *cello*.

The rule in Gaelic spelling is that in a word of more than one syllable, if the last vowel of one syllable is broad, the first vowel of the next syllable must be broad too, e.g. **seòmar**, 'room'. Like must be followed by like on either side of the intervening consonant(s). If the last vowel is slender, the first

---

1. Compare the vowel order in Ogham (an early form of Gadelic script):

-I-	-I-I-	-I-I-I-	-I-I-I-I-	-I-I-I-I-I-
A	O	U	E	I

of the next syllable must be slender too, e.g. **caileag**, 'girl'. There is a good reason for all this. As we have seen, a broad vowel can give a consonant a different sound from a slender vowel, whether before or after the consonant. Thus the 's' sound (as in English 'say') of **cas**, 'foot' and **sàil**, 'heel', but the 'sh' sound (as in English 'ship') of **ris**, 'to' and **sin**, 'that'. As a result, it would be confusing if a consonant were to be flanked by a broad vowel on one side and a slender vowel on the other. With a combination of, say . . . **ase** . . . it would not be clear how the 's' was to be pronounced. When the Gaelic spelling rule is followed there is no confusion with this and the other consonants. If there is no consonant between the vowels then the rule obviously doesn't apply – e.g. **dèan**, 'do'.

Behind the spelling rule (to which there are a few exceptions, notably past participles) lies ease of pronunciation which has adapted words in such a way that the rule simply reflects the sounds produced by the speakers of the language.

From the above it is clear that vowels are often found in a word in conformity with the rule and may not have an actual sound of their own. This is one of the reasons why Gaelic words sometimes seem rather long and full of unpronounced letters. Take the word 'pibroch' for instance. This is obviously an English spelling, since Gaelic would not allow the slender 'i' and the broad 'o' to flank the consonants. So the Gaelic spelling is made up as follows: **pìob**, 'a pipe'; **pìobair**, 'a piper'; **pìobaireachd**, 'piping'. 12 letters in Gaelic, 7 in English! Yet the pronunciation of both words is roughly similar – indeed, 'pibroch' is intended to be an English phonetic spelling of **pìobaireachd**.

Most consonants have a different sound when they are in conjunction with a broad, or a slender, vowel. The most striking cases are D, L, S, and T.

D with a slender vowel is like English 'j', or the initial sound of 'dew', 'due' etc. as pronounced in Scotland (but not, as a rule, in America) e.g. **Diùra** 'Jura'.

D with a broad vowel is closer to English 'd', e.g. **dol**, 'going'.

L with a slender vowel is like English 'li' in 'pavilion', e.g. **leth**, 'half'.

L with a broad vowel is rather like English 'l' in 'although', e.g. **latha**, 'day'.

S has already been mentioned. An easy way for learners to remember its 'soft' sound with a slender vowel is to relate it to an example well-known outside the Gaelic world – as in the pronunciation of the first-name Sean (now frequently anglicised as Shaun).

T with a slender vowel is like English 'ch', or like the initial sound of 'tune', 'Tuesday' etc again as pronounced in Scotland e.g. **teth**, 'hot'.

T with a broad vowel is closer to English 't', e.g. **tarbh**, 'bull'.

These traditional Gaelic spelling conventions with 'd' 't' and 's' have sometimes been disregarded to accommodate the increasing use of English words in the language, especially when they appear at the start of a word. Thus with **teilebhisean** (television) the 't' is not pronounced according to Gaelic rules (which would have meant that the word started with the English sound 'ch'), but as in English spelling rules; the rest of the word is in Gaelic spelling, of course. Or again **seaptaic** (septic), where the 's' is non-Gaelic (traditional Gaelic pronunciation would have given the English sound 'sh') but rather an English 's'; again the rest of the word is in Gaelic spelling, with the 't' flanked by broad vowels (unlike in the English septic) to keep the hard 't' sound. It has to be said, though, that such Gaelic spellings, where the vowels have to be changed in order to preserve a particular consonantal sound, such as the hard 't' in **comataidh** (committee), do not look too convincing from the vowel pronunciation viewpoint.

But this does not always happen. **Dìnnear** (dinner) is borrowed from English but the 'd' is pronounced according to Gaelic conventions i.e. like English 'j'. Similarly – with other borrowings from English – the 'd' in **dèilig** (deal), the 't' in **teadhar** (tether) and so on. The likely explanation relates to the time when a word was introduced into Gaelic. In earlier centuries the widespread monolingualism would ensure that a word borrowed from English would follow Gaelic sound patterns/schemes; in more recent times a bilingual population would more readily accept an English sound pattern.

In view of the above points the modern pronunciation can shed light on the background of a word in Gaelic. For instance **simplidh**, (simple) which looks as if it might have been borrowed from English, has the soft English 'sh' sound at the beginning, which is the traditional Gaelic sound for 's' with a slender vowel. This suggests that it is not borrowed from English, but is rather from the general Indo- European background, or from Latin; so, probably an early borrowing. Contrast this with a more recent borrowing such as **sinc(e)** 'a sink', where the 's' is hard, as in the English word.

We also have to consider the likelihood that under the overbearing presence and pressure of English, words borrowed from English will have changed their pronunciation from a Gaelic to an English format over the centuries.

The main point to bear in mind, then, is that different languages, Gaelic included, can use letters of the alphabet in different ways to represent different sounds. For instance, the letter 'j' has different sounds in English, German, French and

Spanish. So it is not surprising that Bonnie Prince Charlie's name may not look too familiar in Gaelic, since it cannot begin with the letters 'Ch'. These two letters in Gaelic give the guttural sound found in 'lo*ch*'; the required sound, as indicated above, is achieved instead by using the letter 't' with a slender vowel, giving **Teàrlach**.

It has sometimes been suggested that Gaelic would be rather easier to read if it were written phonetically. There have been instances of this in the past, and Manx Gaelic, which is now being successfully revived and is quite close to Scottish Gaelic, is written phonetically. Welsh does this to an extent also, e.g. the lenited form of *mawr* (big – Gaelic **mòr**) is written *fawr*. There are advantages and disadvantages to such a system. The spelling *fawr* makes it easier for someone unfamiliar with the language to pronounce it reasonably correctly (remembering that a Welsh single 'f' has a 'v' sound like English 'of'). But the fact that this is the same word as *mawr* is not immediately obvious to someone who does not know Welsh or another Celtic language; after all, there is no connection between the English words 'more' and 'fore'. Gaelic is the other way round; the spelling conventions have to be learnt before a beginner can make any sort of accurate pronunciation of **mhòr.** But the fact that it is the same word as **mòr** is pretty obvious.

But there are objections. The phonetic scheme suggested is, of course, always English-based, which hardly seems a forward step. But above all, the etymology of the word is destroyed. Consider the word **Didòmhnaich**, 'Sunday'. In this word the lenited 'm' is silent – in no way unusual, as we have seen.[2]

---

2. The 'm' retains its influence, however, by making the preceding 'o' nasal. Gaelic makes considerable use of nasal vowels.

So **dòmhnaich** sounds rather like 'dawnich' or 'donich'. But with the 'm' retained in the Gaelic spelling we can see the cognate, Latin *dominus*, 'lord', 'master', Scots *dominie*, and thus the word obviously means 'the Lord's Day'. So correct spellings can be a help in remembering the meaning of a word.

In this connection it is interesting to note that certain products, e.g. whisky, are now being marketed in Gaelic spelling to give a touch of authenticity, romance, mystery etc. Previously the belief was that calling a product **glè mhath**, 'very good', for instance, might have restricted sales unless it was written in the English phonetic pronunciation Glayva.

Lenition has been changing the sounds and spellings of Gaelic words for centuries, and while this often hinders the recognition of a Gaelic word when it is spoken – e.g. **bùth**, 'shop', is English 'booth', but the 'th' is silent in Gaelic[3] – it is sometimes the English word which is at fault, so to speak. Thus the pronunciation of English 'psalm' with the 'l' silent disguises its identity with Gaelic **salm** (pronounced 'salam').

In many cases, especially with words borrowed from English, an unpronounced lenited consonant is inserted simply to separate syllables, or to end a word. For instance, **staidhre** is the Gaelic spelling of English 'stair' and **pàigh** the Gaelic spelling of 'pay'. The lenited consonants most used in this way are 'bh', 'dh', 'gh', and 'th'.

---

3. English 'th' is not now a used Gaelic sound, although the Hebridean pronunciation of an 'r' with slender vowel (another Norse influence) comes near to it.

VOCABULARY

GAELIC	ENGLISH	ENGLISH COGNATE
airgead	silver, money	argent
bàth	drown	*bath*ymeter
beannachd	blessing, farewell	benediction
cead	permission	cede
dìreach	straight, exact	direct
easbaig	bishop	*episc*opal
feasgar	evening	vesper
glas	lock	clasp
mair	last, endure	*mor*atorium
òsda	hotel	hostel
pòs	marry	spouse
roth	wheel	*rot*ate
saoghal	world	*secul*ar
tràill	slave	thrall

Some place names derived from words mentioned in this chapter.

Tarbh – Bull
Tarfside (Angus)

Leth – Half, Side
Lephinmore (Cowal)
Dandaleith (Moray)

Mòr – Big
Strathmore (Angus)
Aviemore (Invernessshire)

Cìr – Comb, Crest
Cir Mhor (Arran)

CHAPTER 4
INFLECTION

G AELIC is an inflected language. An inflected language is one in which nouns and adjectives change their form according to whether they are the subject of a sentence, or the object, or some other case. Modern English has largely lost its inflections, but the pronouns 'I', 'he', 'she', 'we' and 'they' illustrate the point; in Standard English they can only be used when they are the subject. When they are the object we use 'me', 'him', 'her', 'us' and 'them'. In Gaelic it is the nouns and adjectives which change – although there is no longer a separate objective case – and this provides a further difficulty for learners.

Oddly enough the *pronouns* in modern Gaelic do not change, so that **mi** is both 'I' (subject) and 'me' (object), **sinn** is both 'we' and 'us', and so on. It is curious that the Celtic languages have lost the 'I' form found in the other European language families – 'I' (English), *ich* (German), *io* (Italian) etc. Much the same has happened with the modern English plural 'you', which was originally objective case but is now used as the subject also. Given that there is now only the one form in Gaelic for subject and object pronouns, it would have been equally strange if the subject form had survived and was now used as the object.

This Gaelic use of **mi** as the subject has an interesting echo in some older forms of Indo-European languages, where the ending *-mi* is found as the 'I' form of the verb. So Classical Greek has *didomi* = I give. This *mi* is thought to be the pronoun coming after the verb, as in Gaelic (see chapter 6) – though **written** Gaelic does not, of course, attach it to the verb as Greek did, but when spoken there is little difference.

Living languages are, of course, changing all the time and inflection is a typical feature of them in their earlier stages. Thus Latin is heavily inflected, but most of the modern languages derived from it – e.g. French, Italian, Spanish and Portuguese – have done away with such changes in the word.[1]

Some other modern languages which are still inflected, e.g. Greek, have fewer changes in words than they used to have. Gaelic too has fewer. In its earlier form Gadelic (the ancestor of Gaelic, Irish and Manx) there were five different forms of a noun in the singular, and another five in the plural. Modern Gaelic is much simpler, as we shall see, especially Lewis Gaelic (see the end of chapter 7).

The main difficulty in Gaelic is the genitive case, which is the 'of' form of a word. **Clach**, for instance, is 'stone'; if we wish to say 'of a stone', the form is **cloiche**.[2]

It corresponds, then, to the English possessive case 'stone's'. Unfortunately for learners there is no single way of forming the genitive in Gaelic; rather, there are several groups of words in which the genitive is formed in the same way. However, the position can be simplified to an extent. The majority of nouns insert an 'i' in the genitive, as with **clach,** (quoted above), or, e.g. **fir**, the genitive of **fear**, 'man', and

---

1. Romanian, however, is still partially inflected.

2. The connection between the two different cases may not always be apparent to beginners. For instance in the place names **An t-Allt Beithe** (Aultbea – the stream of the birch tree) and **Taigh an Uillt** (Taynuilt – the house of the stream) **allt** and **uillt** are the same word, the latter simply being the genitive form, 'of the stream'.

the existing vowel(s) is frequently modified. In origin this 'i' is the same as that found in the Latin genitive *domini* (of the lord). In Gadelic too it forms the last letter of the word. In modern Gaelic, however, it has affected the interior of the word. This brings to mind the curious feature of English spelling where the vowel 'e' is used to change the sound of a previous vowel, though a consonant lies between them, as in 'cap; cape', 'cut; cute' etc. The outcome in Gaelic, particularly with the letters 'd', 't' and 's', is a softening of the otherwise hard final consonant, as explained in the previous chapter. Thus **bàs**, 'death' (pronounced baass); **bàis**, 'of death' (pronounced baash).

A noun may also have a final 'e' in the genitive, as in **cloiche** above, and some nouns have a final 'a', e.g. **gutha**, 'of a voice'. This again reflects typical Indo-European inflection. Finally, the corollary of the 'i' inserted to indicate the genitive is that if a word has an 'i' in it already then in many cases the genitive removes that 'i', e.g. **sùil**, 'eye', **sùla**, 'of an eye'.

Adjectives also form their genitive by inserting an 'i', with an additional final 'e' in feminine cases.

However, the genitive is not as widely used as it used to be, particularly in colloquial Gaelic. For instance, although the genitive of **obair**, 'work', is **obrach** (a further class of genitives!) it is not always used in everyday speech. The strict use of many genitives is often felt to be an indication of learned, 'correct' speech, formal and educated, a feature of written Gaelic, for example. This falling out of use of many genitives varies according to locality, and to the 'standing' and age of the speaker, with the older generation tending to preserve them. Indeed, a word such as **dibhe**, the genitive of **deoch**, 'drink', would not only seldom be used colloquially, but would be quite unfamiliar to many younger speakers. All this is perfectly understandable, and, indeed, inevitable. Gaelic is simply following the tendency which has already taken place in other European languages, and continuing its process of simplification. In the case of the genitive this process is assisted by the increasing use of the word **de**, 'of' which does away with the need for a separate genitive form.

The other cases are much simpler. The so-called dative case is the name given to the form of the noun used after prepositions – 'in', 'on', 'at', 'to' etc. In this case the first letter of the noun is lenited if it is 'b', 'c', 'g', 'm' or 'p', otherwise there is no change.[3]

Thus **bòrd**, 'table', **air a' bhòrd**, 'on the table'. This applies to both masculine and feminine nouns, except that feminine nouns generally use the lenited genitive form (minus the final 'e'), e.g. **bròg**, 'shoe', **air a' bhròig**, 'on the shoe'. As we have seen, however, there can be a reluctance to acknowledge an inflected form, so although **clann**, 'children', for example, has the genitive form **cloinne**, one is just as likely to hear **leis a' chlann**, 'with the children' as the more correct **leis a' chloinn**.

In the vocative case, the form used when someone is addressed directly, the first letter of the noun is again lenited, e.g. **a Mhàiri**, 'Mairi!' With masculine names the genitive form (the one with an 'i' in it) is lenited, thus **a Sheumais**, 'Seumas!'

There are two main ways of forming the plural in Gaelic –

a) by adding -**an** or -**ean** (spelling rule!) to the singular, e.g. **làmh**, 'hand', **làmhan**, 'hands'; both masculine and feminine nouns do so. This plural ending in -n has an interest-

---

3. Unless the word begins with 's' – see next chapter.

ing echo in the Germanic languages. It is one of the plural endings in German, and still occasionally retained in modern English (oxen, children) and Scots (*een*, *shoon*).

b) many masculine nouns have a plural form like the genitive singular, i.e. with an inserted 'i', e.g. **each**, 'horse', **eich**, 'horses'. This is rather like English monosyllables such as 'mouse', 'foot', etc. with their plurals 'mice', 'feet', where a slender vowel(s) replaces the broad vowel(s) of the singular. Sometimes both forms of plurals are used with the same word in different districts; thus **dealbh**, 'picture', for instance, has the plurals **dealbhan** and **deilbh**.

There is also a quite distinct plural which involves the addition of the ending **-(a)ichean**, e.g. **litir**, 'letter', **litrichean**, 'letters'. This form is frequently used in modern words borrowed from English, so that one hears **busaichean**, 'buses', **loidhnichean**, 'lines'.

VOCABULARY

GAELIC	ENGLISH	ENGLISH COGNATE
àirneis	furniture, fittings	harness
beò	living	*bio*logy
ceangal	tie, connect	*cinct*ure
donn	brown	dun
eile	other	alien
fèileadh	kilt	veil
gobhal	fork	gable
a-màireach	tomorrow	morrow
peacadh	sin	im*pecc*able
prìomh	first	prime

ruadh	red	ruddy
sean	old	*sen*ile
taigh	house	*teg*ula, thatch
uisge	water	whisky (water of life)

Some place names derived from words mentioned in this chapter.

Clach – Stone
Achnacloiche (Argyll; Skye; Ross and Cromarty)
Clackmannan (Central Region)

Donn – Brown
Tomdoun (Glengarry)

Ruadh – Red
Roy Bridge (Invernessshire)

Sean – Old
Shanwell (Kinross)

Taigh – House
Tighnabruaich (Cowal)
Tyndrum (Perthshire)

Uisge – Water
Loch Uisg (Mull)

CHAPTER 5
LETTERS LOST OR ADDED, STRESS AND ACCENT

WE HAVE already seen how Gaelic pronunciation some-times disguises the connection of a word with its English cognate, and how the similarity is clearer when the word is written down. In some cases, however, the written form of the word needs an explanation before we can see the connection. Gaelic treatment of the letter 'p' is an example. Early Gaelic did not reproduce this 'p' sound which was present in other European languages, particularly at the beginning of words. Thus the Latin *pater*, 'father', takes the forms *padre*, *père*, 'paternal' in Italian, French and English, but the Gaelic form is **athair**. This feature is, on the face of it, such a curious phenomenon that it is reassuring to find it elsewhere in the Indo-European family of languages. Armenian provides many parallels with Gaelic; for instance Gaelic **athair** is Armenian *hayr*. (Note that apart from the missing 'p' the internal 't' sound has also vanished, as in Gaelic and French.)

Bearing this loss of 'p' in mind we can see the connection between the following:

GAELIC	ENGLISH	ENGLISH COGNATE
ùr	new, fresh	pure
eun	bird	pen (i.e. quill)
iasg	fish	piscivorous, Pisces
làn	full	plentiful
leathann	broad	platypus

sir	search	speir (Scots)
uircean	piglet	porcine

Sometimes the 'p' is missing inside the word:

teth	hot	tepid
caora	sheep	Capricorn

Sometimes the 'p' is replaced by another consonant:

seachd	seven	septet

Present day Gaelic words which begin with 'p' are not original, but have been borrowed, mainly from Latin, French and English. This early absence of 'p' is, of course, what lies behind the traditional description of Gaelic (with Irish and Manx) as a 'q' Celtic language, as opposed to Welsh, Breton and Cornish, which are 'p' Celtic.

In Gaelic 'q' is written 'c' (hard, like 'k'), and the related word in Welsh, etc will have a 'p' instead – so Kintyre : **Ceann Tìre**: Headland, is Pentire in Cornwall. There are many instances of this p/q interchange which also continued later when Gaelic borrowed words from Latin. So, for instance, Latin *pascha*, 'easter' is Gaelic **càisg**. This phenomenon is not confined to the Celtic languages; consider 'cashmere' and 'pashmina' at the other side of the Indo-European world.

Learners should also be aware, however, that modern Gaelic uses the letter 'b' to produce the sound of 'p', provided that 'b' is not the first letter of the word; that is, the 'b' is unvoiced. So **obair**, 'work' is pronounced like *opair*, and indeed was so written in Old Irish.[1] This less resonant pronunciation of a consonant occurs with the letters 'b', 'd' and 'g' when they end a word after a vowel, or are in the middle of a word flanked by vowels (as in **obair** above); in such cases they are

---

1. There is still occasionally some fluidity; **leabaidh** 'bed', for instance, usually has **leapa** as its genitive.

unvoiced, i.e. sounded like 'p', 't' and 'c' respectively. So **bog** 'soft', 'moist', **gob** 'beak', and **rud** 'thing' are pronounced as if their last letters were 'c', 'p' and 't'. This is a fairly common linguistic phenomenon. English, for instance, sounds the final 'd' of the past tense of verbs as a 't' if the previous consonant is unvoiced (i.e. 'f', 'k', 'p', 's'). So the 'd' of 'helped' is sounded like a 't', and so on. Scots regularly sounds and writes an English final 'd' as a 't'; for instance *crookit*, but English 'crooked'; and unvoiced consonants in Latin are frequently voiced in its Romance derivatives, as Latin *pater* (father) but Italian (and English !) *padre*, Latin *ficus* (fig) but French *figue*, Spanish *higo*, etc.[2] This is also a feature of German, where 'b', 'd' and 'g' are unvoiced at the end of a word.

There are, of course, good reasons why Gaelic does not spell these words *boc, gop*, and *rut*. In writing (though not in speech) it could introduce unnecessary confusion since **boc**, for example, is a quite different word, meaning 'a buck – a male goat, deer etc'. As regards speech, words ending with 'c' after a vowel usually, but not always, have the sound *chk*, for which the Gaelic orthography is **chd**. So **breac** 'speckled' has a *chk* sound at the end; indeed, it was sometimes spelled **breachd**, though this spelling has fallen out of use. Final 'p' and 't' after a vowel generally have preaspiration, giving *hp* and *ht* sounds as mentioned in chapter 2. So changing the endings of such words to accommodate English spelling conventions would give the wrong sounds in Gaelic.

There is also the well-known instance of the disappearance of the letter yogh in English as it was written and printed in Scotland. This yogh had the sound of a consonantal 'y', as in English 'yes' and in form rather resembled the number 3, or

---

2. *Higo* also provides an example of the disappearance of the sound 'f' mentioned in connection with Gaelic lenited 'f' in chapter 2.

the downward shape of a handwritten 'z'. When printing, as opposed to writing, in Scots and English began in Scotland, yogh did not get a separate letter shape but was assigned the letter 'z', which was judged to resemble the shape of yogh most closely. So Gaelic words like **MacCoinnich** were transliterated into English as MacKenzie, originally pronounced MacKenyie, with the yogh (i.e. the 'z') representing the 'y' sound found in Gaelic **nn** (which is pronounced 'ny'). Today, of course, MacKenzie is pronounced (wrongly but understandably) with the English 'z' sound, thus obscuring its Gaelic connection. Another surname, Menzies, whose 'z' is also a yogh, is rapidly going the same way.

Another factor is metathesis, which refers to consonants changing places within a word, as in the two English forms 'girdle' and 'griddle'. Thus in Gaelic **còisir**, 'choir' is from 'chorus', **susbaint** from 'substance', and **seanailear** from 'general' (rank).[3]

Sometimes, in addition to this interchange of consonants there is also a missing 'p' to take into account; thus **làmh**, 'hand' is cognate with 'palm', and **baist** with 'baptize'.

Yet another factor concerns masculine nouns which begin with a vowel, and feminine nouns (and masculine in some cases) which begin with an 's'. Such words have a 't' inserted between themselves and the definite article, e.g. **an t-ìm**, 'the butter', **an t-sràid**, 'the street'. In the latter instance the 's' is not pronounced. Consider the name Macintyre, which means 'son of the joiner, carpenter' (**saor**). The Gaelic form is **Mac an t-Saoir**.

---

3. The form of **seanailear** may also be influenced by the ending -**air** which is used in Gaelic to describe an agent, someone who does something, e.g. **iasgair**, 'fisherman', **sealgair**, 'hunter'.

This insertion of the letter 't' has the potential to cause some uncertainty for beginners, since in spoken Gaelic there is a similarity of sound between such words and other, different, words which **actually** begin with a 't'. Thus **an t-ìm**, mentioned above, sounds like **an tìm**, 'the time'; likewise **an t-àl**, 'the offspring, brood' and **an tàl**, 'the adze', **an t-eas**, 'the waterfall' and **an teas**, 'the heat', and so on. While beginners need to be alert to this, in practice the context usually makes things clear, just as, to take a rather similar feature in English, 'an ale' is unlikely to be confused with 'a nail'. Returning to **Mac** names, readers should be aware that in Gaelic, unlike in English, these are only used of males. Gaelic therefore avoids the apparent incongruity of English-type names such as Mary Donald**son**; instead it uses the word **Nic**, probably a combination of **nighean**, 'daughter' and **mac**, 'son', so Mary Donaldson is **Màiri NicDhòmhnaill**. Such a distinction is, of course, common in the Slav languages and is even found in the Germanic language family. The use of *dottir* (i.e. daughter) in Icelandic, e.g. Gudrun Karlsdottir, is a bit like the Gaelic way, except that the Icelandic surname is liable to change with each generation.

In some cases in Gaelic the 't' has become attached by analogy to a word borrowed from another language; thus **tiota**, 'a moment', 'a little', is from Greek/Latin 'iota', 'a jot'. If the foreign word began with an 'h'('h' being mainly a sign of lenition in Gaelic and not a letter in its own right) then the same thing could happen; thus **talla**, 'hall', **taigeis**, 'haggis', **togsaid**, 'hogshead'.[4]

The influence of lost letters is also related to the question

---

4. Compare, in English, the words 'adder' (originally 'nadder' – Gaelic **nathair**, 'snake') and 'orange' (which also originally began with 'n'). The converse, which also happens in Gaelic, is seen in words like 'newt', originally 'ewt'.

of stress and accent. The stress in Gaelic falls on the first syllable of the word no matter how long the word may be, e.g. **ath**arrachadh, 'change'; apparent exceptions, such as **airson**, 'for', which is stressed on the second syllable, are really two words – in this case **air son**, 'on account (of)'. Until fairly recently two accents were used, the grave ` and the acute ´. These are placed above long vowels which have a stress. In such cases 'a', 'u' and 'i' always had a grave accent, e.g. **fàs**, 'grow', **cìr**, 'comb', **ùr**, 'new'.

A grave accent above 'o' and 'e' indicated the 'open' sound of these vowels, i.e. like 'o' and 'e' in English 'form' and 'herd', e.g. **òr**, 'gold', **cè**, 'cream'. An acute accent over 'o' and 'e' indicated the 'closed' sound of these vowels, as in English 'more' and 'rein', e.g; **có**?, 'who?', **dé**?, 'what?'. There is a growing tendency, however, to do away with the acute accent and to use only the grave instead, as recommended in the recent (1981) reform of Gaelic spelling.

The accent is useful in written Gaelic to distinguish words which would otherwise have the same spelling. Some common instances are:

aithne	knowledge	**àithne**	commandment
am	the	**àm**	time
ath	next	**àth**	ford (m), kiln (f)
bas	palm (of hand)	**bàs**	death
bata	a stick	**bàta**	boat
bith	existence	**bìth**	gum, glue
brath	spying	**bràth**	judgement
caraid	friend	**càraid**	pair, couple
caise	short temper	**càise**	cheese
dail	dale	**dàil**	delay

de of	**dè?** what?
fad length	**fàd** a peat
faisg near	**fàisg** press, squeeze
feith wait	**fèith** sinew
gabhadh let (him, etc) take	**gàbhadh** danger
gun without	**gùn** gown
sabaid fight	**Sàbaid** Sunday
samhach a handle	**sàmhach** quiet
sin that	**sìn** stretch
rudan things	**rùdan** a knuckle

Of course the context usually makes it clear which word is meant.

In many Gaelic words the stressed long vowel with accent compensates for a consonant lost from Indo-European, as can be seen from the English cognate, e.g. **cìs**, 'tax' (ce*n*sus),[5] **mìos**, 'month' (me*n*sual). In fact, many long vowels and diphthongs are there to compensate for a lost consonant, e.g. **neul**, 'cloud' (ne*b*ulous), **ceud**, 'hundred' (ce*n*tury).

An accent is also used to indicate that the stress is not in its traditional place (on the first syllable of a Gaelic word) but is somewhere else in the word, when the word in question is borrowed from another language, usually English. This indicates that the position of the stress in the other language is retained, but the vowel is not necessarily long; thus **buntàta**, 'potato', **tomàto**, 'tomato'. A traditional Gaelic word starting in a similar way – e.g. **tomadach**, 'bulky' – can be assumed to have its stress on the first syllable, the norm in Gaelic, and only needs an accent if that first syllable/vowel is long (which it isn't in this case).

---

5. Compare also English 'excise'.

Sometimes, however, the accent does not reflect the borrowed word; **modaràtor**, for instance, obviously has its stress on the third syllable, yet the English word behind it, (which explains the non-Gaelic spelling **moderàtor** sometimes found) 'moderator' (of the Kirk), is stressed on the first syllable. All of this is in marked contrast to the procedure in earlier centuries, where the stress accent of a foreign word borrowed into Gaelic was moved to accommodate the Gaelic norm – i.e. moved to the first syllable. So **easbaig**, 'bishop', though Classical Greek/Latin *episcopus*, from which it is derived, has the stress on the second syllable. Likewise **eaglais**, 'church' from Classical Greek/Latin *ecclesia*, **deisciobal**, 'disciple' from Latin *discipulus*, and so on. Nowadays the all-pervasive influence of English has made such a change unnecessary, although **poileas,** 'police' is a curious throwback, possibly influenced by Central Belt Scots.

VOCABULARY

GAELIC	ENGLISH	ENGLISH COGNATE
anam	soul	*anim*ate
bò	cow	*bo*vine
borb	fierce	*barb*arian
ceart	right	*cert*ain
ceil	hide	con*ceal*
èirich	rise	erect
fìon	wine	vine
marbh	dead	*morb*id
ràmh	oar	tri*reme*
sabhal	barn	stable
sàl	sea	*sal*ine

sgillinn	penny	shilling (old Scots)
sgìre	district	shire
trang	busy	throng

Some place names derived from words mentioned in this chapter:

Leathann – Broad
Glen Lean (Cowal)

Eun – Bird
Loch nan Eun (Lochnagar; North Uist)

Saor – Joiner
Blantyre (Lanarkshire)

Àth – Ford
Acharacle (Moidart)

Dail – Field
Dull (Perthshire)
Dalwhinnie (Invernessshire)

Fada – Long
Loch Fad (Bute)
Ben Attow (Inverness/Ross and Cromarty border)

Ràmh – Oar
Dunderave (Argyll)

Sabhal – Barn
Tomintoul (Banffshire)

Sàl – Sea
Salen (Mull; Ardnamurchan)
Kintail (Ross and Cromarty)

Eas – Waterfall
Bunessan (Mull)
Dalness (Glen Etive)

Ìm – Butter
Ben Ime (Argyll)

CHAPTER 6
SOME PROBLEMS WITH VERBS

THE MAIN difficulties with the verb in Gaelic concern the verb 'to be', the irregular verbs, and the verbal noun, each of which will now be considered.

Like some other languages (e.g. Italian and Spanish), Gaelic has two verbs 'to be', usually referred to by their present tense forms **tha** and **is**. **Tha** ('am', 'is', 'are') is the commoner of the two; its past tense is **bha** ('was', 'were'). The past tense of **is** is **bu.** The two verbs, however, are not directly interchangeable. **Is** is used when we wish to emphasise a particular word in a sentence, and this word follows the verb, e.g. **is mòr mo mhulad**, 'great is my sorrow'. **Tha**, on the other hand, simply makes a statement without any particular emphasis, e.g. **tha mi sgìth**, 'I'm tired'. In addition, **is** is used in certain idiomatic phrases, e.g. **is toigh leam**, 'I like', **is aithne dhomh**, 'I know'. **Tha** should not be used in such instances.

The above phrase **tha mi sgìth** illustrates a fundamental rule of Gaelic word order, that the subject always **follows** its verb, unlike in modern English – 'I'm tired' – where it precedes it. Having the subject after its verb is a feature of German also, provided the verb is not the first word in the sentence. So it is not surprising that English in its earlier stages used to do this too; there are many instances in the seventeenth century translation of the Bible, where a phrase such as 'Then came to him the disciples of John' resembles the Gaelic translation **An sin thàinig deisciobuil Eoin d'a ionnsuidh**.

The twentieth century English translation removes this archaism, of course, and writes 'Then the disciples. . . came.'

Tha is in origin not really a verb of existence but rather indicates state, status or condition, not usually permanent. That is why, for instance, it cannot be used as it stands to indicate the state or occupation of a person, but must have some form of the preposition **ann**, 'in', after it. Thus 'I was a boy' is not **bha mi balach** but rather **bha mi 'nam bhalach. Tha**, which is cognate with Italian *sta* and Spanish *esta*, basically means 'stand', although it is, of course, used as a verb 'to be' in all three languages. Compare Italian *come sta?* 'how are you?' with Gaelic **ciamar a tha (thu)**?

Is, which is obviously related to English 'is', Latin and French *est*, German *ist* etc. is unusual in its sound. The letter 'i' in Gaelic, in monosyllables and stressed syllables, normally has the sound of 'i' in the Romance languages, i.e. the vowel sound in English 'feet', Italian *vino* etc. So Gaelic **mi, tìr** etc. But in **is** it is close to the vowel sound of English 'is'. Also the sound of the 's' is unusual, since we would normally expect the 'sh' sound (as in English 'ship') because of the slender vowel before the 's', as explained in chapter 3.

The verb 'to be' is irregular in most languages and **tha** is no exception. Its question form is **a bheil?** and its negative **chan eil**. The same forms in the past tense are **an robh?** and **cha robh**. The reason for these different forms is simply that they are, in origin, different verbs. Thus, rather than saying that **bha** is the past tense of **tha** we should really say that **bha** is used as the past tense of **tha**, just as in English 'was' is used as the past tense of 'am'. As indicated above, in Gaelic the verb is usually the first word in the sentence, so **tha** is probably the most common start to a Gaelic sentence, particularly since the language has no simple present tense, as English 'I sing', but has to use the form with the verb 'to be', 'I am singing', **tha mi a' seinn**. **Tha** is also used as a single word sentence, meaning 'yes'. This is because Gaelic does not really have words for the simple 'yes' and 'no'; instead, the verb used in the question is repeated. The equivalent in English would be something like 'are you busy?' – 'I am'. Thus to any question beginning 'is?' or 'are?' – using **a bheil**? – the answer in Gaelic is **tha** if we mean 'yes' and **chan eil** if we mean 'no'. In addition **tha** is frequently heard as the equivalent of English 'um', expressing hesitancy in speech.

The verbs 'to be' are also used in Gaelic to get round the fact that the language has no verb 'to have' in its simple form. Instead of saying 'I have a dog' Gaelic uses a phrase corresponding to 'there is a dog at me', **tha cù agam**. **Agam** is for **aig mi** (which is never used) just as in English 'I'd' is for 'I had' or 'I would'. All the personal pronouns have special forms when used with prepositions like **aig**, 'at', **air**, 'on', **do**, 'to' etc., and many of these forms are more complex than mere contractions. Most grammar books give a full table of such forms.

Apart from the verb 'to be', Gaelic has only ten irregular verbs and so compares favourably in this respect with other European languages. As in other languages, it is the most common verbs which are irregular, and so beginners meet them early. Thus **rach**, 'go' has **chaidh**, 'went' as its past tense. In other irregular verbs the different forms have arisen because of the use of prefixes and the alternating of the stress accent between the first and second syllable. Compare the English 'swear' and 'answer'. The latter form is simply 'swear' with the prefix 'an-' (meaning 'in return', 'against') but we can see how placing the stress on the first syllable – '*an*swer' – has affected the sound (and spelling) of the second syllable '-swer', so that it may not be immediately recognised as the verb 'swear'. Gaelic irregular verb forms have been arrived at in a similar way, but the alterations are even greater. Thus in early Gaelic '(he) gets' is **fo-gheibh** where **fo** is the prefix and **gheibh** the verb. The stress was on the second syllable **gheibh**, and as often happens, the unstressed prefix **fo** eventually dropped off. So today 'gets', or rather 'will get'[1] is simply **gheibh**.

Now to ask a question in Gaelic we put **am** or **an** in front of the verb, so 'does (he) get?' or 'will (he) get?' was originally **am fo-gheibh**? In this phrase the stress is again on the second element which this time is **fo**. So again the unstressed end part dropped off, leaving **am fo-gh**? which is, today, **am faigh**?, 'will (he) get?'.

Other irregular verb forms have evolved in similar circumstances. Grammar books give all the different forms.

Participles, or verbal nouns (so called because although verbs, they can be used as nouns, e.g. 'there was much coming and going') are unusual in Gaelic in that there is no one single way of forming them. In English the participle/verbal noun always ends in -ing. In Gaelic there are more than ten different endings and it is really a matter of learning them all individually. The reason for such variety is that Gaelic has made use of different suffixes in the language. We can see that the same thing happened in English, where nouns are formed with the use of various suffixes, e.g.

-ade with 'block' gives 'blockade'

-age with 'bond' gives 'bondage'

-ance with 'annoy' gives 'annoyance'

-er with 'treasure' gives 'treasurer'

---

1. Future forms can sometimes have a present tense feeling in Gaelic.

-cy   with 'bankrupt'   gives   'bankruptcy'

-dom   with 'free'   gives   'freedom'

and so on. In Gaelic the main relevant suffixes are **-(e)adh**, **-t**, **-ail** or **-eil**, **-t(a)inn**, **-sinn**, **-eachd**, **-aidh**, **-se**, **-(e)amh**; the spelling rule determines the precise form. Most of the participles are formed with one of these suffixes attached to the root, which in Gaelic is the imperative. Thus whereas English has used suffixes to form nouns, Gaelic has used them to form verbal nouns.

The most common suffix is **-(e)adh**, e.g. **a' bualadh**, 'striking', from **buail**, 'strike'. This is also the form used in Gaelic words taken from English, e.g. **a' smocadh**, 'smoking', **a' fònadh**, 'phoning'. This form is also used in some dialects where 'standard' Gaelic has a different form; thus **a' dèanamh**, 'doing', has the form **a' dèanadh** in Islay. Such variation is not untypical; there is often more than one form of the same participle. So 'saying', for example, may be **a' cantainn** or **a' cantail**, 'throwing' may be **a' tilgeil** or **a' tilgeadh**.

There are also verbs where the participle/verbal noun has the same form as the root, i.e. there is no change, e.g. **òl**, 'drink', **ag òl**, 'drinking', **ruith**, 'run', **a' ruith**, 'running'. Most grammar books and dictionaries give all the participle forms, since there is otherwise no way in which the learner can become familiar with them.

Infinitives (the English form 'to open') are the same as the participles/verbal nouns, but with the first letter lenited if possible. Thus **dùin**, 'shut', **a' dùnadh**, 'shutting', **a dhùnadh**, 'to shut'. If the verb begins with a vowel or 'f', then **dh** (as in the past tense – see chapter 2) is placed before the verb, e.g. **innis**, 'tell', **a dh'innse**, 'to tell', **fosgail**, 'open', **a dh'fhosgladh**, 'to open'.

VOCABULARY

GAELIC	ENGLISH	ENGLISH COGNATE
adhradh	worship	ad*ore*
bòrd	table	board
broc	badger	brock
calman	dove	columbine, Columba
capall	mare	*caval*ry
clag	bell	clock
coinean	rabbit	coney
fìor	true	*veri*ly, *veri*fy
mil	honey	*mell*ifluous
salach	dirty	sallow
seac	wither	de*sicc*ate
sgadan	herring	shad
speur	sky	sphere

Some place names derived from words mentioned in this chapter.

Cù – Dog
Balgone (East Lothian)
Camusnacon (Kinlochleven)

Broc – Badger
Ibrox (Glasgow)

Capall – Mare, Horse
Drumchapel (Glasgow)
Inverchapel (Cowal)

Sgadan – Herring
Garscadden (Glasgow)

CHAPTER 7
DIALECTS

LIKE OTHER languages, Gaelic has its share of dialects. This can be a problem for learners. There is still really no 'standard' Gaelic in the same way as there is 'standard' English. Each area has its own form of Gaelic, which can, on occasions, provide difficulties for someone from another area. Such diversity, with its consequent enrichment of the language, is a welcome feature of a living tongue. A dialect form can even, on occasions, make life easier for learners.

Dhèan, 'made', 'did', the form of the past tense found in Islay and elsewhere, is a case in point. This form, made in the normal past tense way, is easier to grasp than the apparently irregular **rinn**, which is the standard past tense. Such occurrences are a feature of dialects of a language. An instance in English is 'went', from the seldom-used verb 'to wend', used as the irregular past tense of 'go'; Scots uses the regular *gaed* for the past tense. Beginners in the language, however, need some sort of standard form to learn. In previous centuries a non-Gaelic speaker who wished to learn Gaelic could simply go to a particular area of the Highlands and Islands and learn the language there. He or she was greatly helped in this by the extensive monoglot nature of many areas. Today, teaching aids mean that anyone can learn the language without necessarily setting foot in a Gaelic-speaking area. Indeed, the now universal bilingualism there can be quite an impediment.

Thus there is an advantage in using a 'standard' form of

Gaelic as far as possible and such a standard is gradually evolving. Education is also a factor, e.g. Gaelic as a school examination subject. The broadcasting of Gaelic on radio and television has also helped, in that professional broadcasters are aware that they are speaking to all of the Gaidhealtachd – and beyond – and therefore tend to exclude extreme forms of dialect of their own particular area. But, it must be stressed, it is only the more extreme provincialisms which are avoided in such cases, and it is still clear from a broadcaster's speech where he or she comes from. For most native speakers, however, – the man in the croft – 'standard' Gaelic is at best a shadowy notion, and when speaking they will use the dialect of their own area. There will be exceptions to this, though, in more formal situations. The well-known Islay song (port-a-beul) **'S ann an Ìle, 'n Ìle, 'n Ìle. . .** (It's in Islay I was born and raised. . .) would, ironically, not normally be sung in Islay dialect by an Islay Gaelic choir.

The position is rather similar to Scots, where there is no agreed standard form. All this has much to do with the fact that Gaelic, always more widely spoken than written, has lacked the status of a national language. Now that Gaelic is being used more extensively in print, there is a further impetus towards a standard form. In the past, dictionaries, for instance, tended to contain provincialisms peculiar to the dialect of the author, sometimes without warning the reader that such was the case. It is only recently, too, that a wholly Gaelic dictionary has appeared; previously Gaelic dictionaries gave the meaning of each Gaelic word in English – i.e. dictionaries were Gaelic-English (and vice-versa) – which speaks volumes for the perceived status of the language and its speakers.

The issue of dialects has been simplified, within the past century, by the regrettable dying out of the language in certain areas, e.g. Perthshire, Strathspey, St. Kilda, Kintyre.

As one might expect, dialect differences belong to two main categories, a) individual words, and b) pronunciation. Some examples of a) are:

> **gealbhan**, the Islay word for 'a fire' (**teine**);
>
> **dar**, mainland Inverness-shire for 'when' (**nuair**);
>
> **Ceusda**, Barra word for 'Easter' (**Càisg**);
>
> **àsan**, Uist form of 'they' (**iadsan**);
>
> **bùrn**, Lewis word for 'water' (**uisge**);
>
> **cneap**, Islay word for 'a button' (**putan**).

Some examples of b) are:

> the sound 'e' for 'a' in Islay, so that **mac**, 'son', sounds like *mec* – or **'s ann** (mentioned above in the song **'S ann an Ìle**) sounds a bit like *sen*;
>
> the Hebridean soft 'r' sounding rather like English 'th', so that **air a' mhuir**, 'on the sea', sounds like *aith a' mhuith*;
>
> the apparent dropping of an initial 'd' in Lewis, so that **an-dè**, 'yesterday', sounds like *an yey*;
>
> final **-(e)amh**, as in **a' dèanamh**, 'doing', pronounced 'oo' (as in English 'foot') in Uist;
>
> the Lewis habit of not sounding the 't' of the article placed before masculine nouns beginning with a vowel, so that **an t-eilean**, 'the island' sounds like *an eilean*.

This last feature at least has the advantage of avoiding possible confusion with words actually beginning with a 't', as mentioned in chapter 5.

There are also differences between the various Gaelic dialects with regard to inflection. In the Gaelic of Lewis, for instance, the different cases of a noun are frequently disregarded, with only the nominative/objective case being used. Thus in Lewis **mullach a' bheinn** – 'the top of the mountain' – is frequently heard in place of the 'standard' **mullach na beinne**. For this reason, although it may dismay purists, Lewis Gaelic could be said to be more advanced than other Scottish Gaelic dialects, since it is further down the road towards minimal inflection, which the history of other European languages suggests will eventually occur in Gaelic too. The language has, of course, already moved considerably in this direction, as a glance at the more complex declensions of Old Irish will show. It becomes even more likely when we realise that there are currently far more speakers of Lewis Gaelic than of any of the other regional dialects in the Highlands and Islands.

VOCABULARY

GAELIC	ENGLISH	ENGLISH COGNATE
aimsir	time	measure
amhairc	look at	mark
buidhe	yellow	bay
bùrn	water	burn
brochan	porridge	broth
can	say	chant
clann	children	clan (borrowed from Gaelic)
croch	hang	*cruc*ify
cruaidh	hard	crude
mion, meanbh	small	*min*or
sgrìobh	write	scribe
sìth	peace	sit (i.e. be inactive)
slaod	drag	slide

Some place names derived from words mentioned in this chapter.

Buidhe – Yellow
Loch Buie (Mull)
Achiltibuie (Ross and Cromarty)

Eadar – Between
Eddrachillis (Sutherland)
Edradynate (Perthshire)
Benderloch (Argyll)

Cruaidh – Hard
Kerrycroy (Bute)

THE USE of time and number in Gaelic differs from that of English in one or two ways. One to ten in Gaelic (with some English cognates) is:

1 **aon** (unit)

2 **dà** (dual) Unlike English, it takes a singular form of the noun, lenited, a relic of the dual case found in old Gaelic (and other European languages); so 'two dogs' is **dà chù**.

3 **trì** (triple)

4 **ceithir** (quatrain)

5 **còig** (quin : 'n' missing in Gaelic – see chapter 5)

6 **sia**

7 **seachd** (septet; no original 'p' in Gaelic)

8 **ochd** (octet)

9 **naoi** (nonary)

10 **deich** (decade)

Unlike English, Gaelic has no independent words for 11 and 12, but says instead 'one ten', 'two ten':

11 **aon deug**

12 **dà dheug**

Note that **deich** takes the form **deug** from 11 onwards, just as English 'ten' changes to 'teen'.

13 **trì deug**, and so on.

20 is **fichead** (English 'vigesimal', French *vingt*). Gaelic continues to use the traditional score system of counting (as do Basque and Danish, and even French provides an instance – as 80 below; the old English use of *score* – e.g. three score years and ten – also provides a parallel; consider too the pound sterling, formerly made up of twenty shillings). So 30 is 'ten on twenty', 40 is 'two twenties' and so on. Thus:

30 **deich air fhichead**

40 **dà fhichead**

50 **dà fhichead 's a deich**

60 **trì fichead**

70 **trì fichead 's a deich**

80 **ceithir fichead** (compare French *quatre vingt*)

90 **ceithir fichead 's a deich**

A 'hundred' is **ceud**; 'fifty' is more often **leth-cheud** (**leth** = half), or **caogad**, a 'thousand' is **mìle** and a 'million' is **millean**.

In naming years Gaelic speakers often prefer to use English because of the rather cumbersome method involved in Gaelic. Thus, for 1983 one must say in Gaelic something corresponding to 'nine hundred ten (i.e. nineteen hundred) four twenties and three' – **naoi ceud deug, ceithir fichead 's a trì,** or sometimes 'a thousand, nine hundred, four twenties and three' – **mìle, naoi ceud, ceithir fichead 's a trì**. Most Gaelic speakers therefore simply say 'nineteen eighty-three'.

In an attempt to avoid the complexities of the score system a decimal system has recently been introduced, with terms based on the already existing **caogad**, 'fifty'. Thus:

30 **trìthead**

40 **ceathrad**

50 **caogad**

60 **seasgad**

70 **seachdad**

80 **ochdad**

90 **naochad**

These are beginning to be heard more often (and they were in fact common in some eastern highland dialects where the language has now died out). But the system of counting in twenties is deeply entrenched, even beyond a hundred (but not 200 and beyond); **sia fichead**, for instance, is commonly heard for 120.

Like English, Gaelic has separate words for 'first', 'second' etc. The ending **-(e)amh** corresponds to English -th.

1st **a' chiad**

2nd **an dara**, or **an dàrna**

3rd **an treas**

4th **an ceathramh**

5th **an còigeamh**

6th **an siathamh**

7th **an seachdamh**

8th **an t-ochdamh**

9th **an naoidheamh**

10th **an deicheamh**

Unlike English, however, Gaelic has a separate set of numerical forms from one to ten, used only of people. Thus 'three persons' in Gaelic is **triùir**. The list is:

aonar   one person

dithis   two persons

triùir	three persons
ceathrar	four persons
còignear	five persons
sianar	six persons
seachdnar	seven persons
ochdnar	eight persons
naoinear	nine persons
deichnear	ten persons

To tell the time in Gaelic we need to know, in addition to the numerals, the following words:

uair	hour
leth-uair	half hour
mionaid	minute
cairteal	quarter
gu	to
an dèidh	after

So, 'twenty past ten' is **fichead mionaid an dèidh a deich**; 'a quarter to eleven' is **cairteal gu aon uair deug**.

The days of the week, which start with the prefix **Di-**, signifying 'day', are mainly named after Roman gods and Celtic fasts. (**aoine** = fast).

Monday **Diluain** (lunar, cf. French *Lundi*)

Tuesday **Dimàirt** (Mars, cf. French *Mardi*)

Wednesday **Diciadain** (first fast day – **ciad aoine**)

Thursday **Diardaoin** (between two fasts – **eadar dà aoine**)

Friday **Dihaoine** (fast day – **aoine**)

Saturday **Disathairne** (Saturn)

Sunday **Didòmhnaich** (*dominus* – lord),
or **Latha na Sàbaid** (Sabbath day)

A 'week' is **seachdain** (**seachd** = seven) and a 'fortnight'
is **cola-deug,** from **còig latha deug** – inclusive counting, as
in many other European languages.

There are Gaelic names for the months of the year, given
in all grammars, but they are seldom used by native speakers,
for good historical reasons. In a sense the use of the names is
artificial in that they do not refer to specific months but rather
to certain periods and events of the year. For instance
Gearran, 'February' is the gelding time, which was not
necessarily restricted to the four weeks of February. The Gaelic
names are increasingly used, however, as exact equivalents of
the English months; grammar books give the complete list.

The seasons are **Earrach**, 'Spring', **Samhradh**, 'Summer',
Foghar, 'Autumn' and **Geamhradh**, 'Winter'.

Some other days which have Gaelic names are:

Bealltainn	May Day, Beltane
A' Bhliadhn' Ùr	New Year
A' Chàisg	Easter
An Nollaig	Xmas
Oidhche Challainn	Hogmanay
Oidhche Shamhna	Hallowe'en

VOCABULARY

GAELIC	ENGLISH	ENGLISH COGNATE
àrd	high	*ard*uous
bròg	shoe	brogue
buachaille	herdsman	*bucol*ic

comann	society	*community*
creag	rock	crag
creid	believe	creed
cridhe	heart	*cardiac*
ionga	claw	unguis
muir	sea	mere, *marine*
stad	stop	*station*
stang	pool, ditch	stagnant
sùlaire	gannet	*solan* goose

Some place names derived from words mentioned in this chapter.

Dà – Two
Dunderave (Argyll)
Dandaleith Moray)

Àrd – High
Ardlui (Dumbartonshire)
Ardentinny (Cowal)

Buachaille – Herdsman
Buachaille Etive Mòr (Glencoe)

Creag – Rock
Craignure (Mull)
Craigmillar (Edinburgh)

Sùlaire – Solan Goose
Sulasgeir (50 miles NW of Cape Wrath)

Ceathramh – Fourth, a Quarter
Pitkerro (Dundee)
Kerrycroy (Bute)

PLACE NAMES in Gaelic are of three main types:

1. The Gaelic is much the same as the English, usually because the English form is simply an approximate rendering of the Gaelic sound, conforming to English spelling conventions. Thus **Tom an t-Sabhail** ('the hillock of the barn') is Tomintoul, **Bogha Mòr** ('big submerged sea rock') is Bowmore.

2. The Gaelic and English are translations of each other, and so one obviously needs some knowledge of Gaelic to understand this type. Some examples are:

An t-Àth Leathann	Broadford
An Eaglais Bhreac	Falkirk (speckled – Scots *faw* – church)[1]
Bail' Ùr an t-Slèibh	Newtonmore (new town on the moor)
Ceann Loch Gilb	Lochgilphead

3. The Gaelic name is quite different from the English,

---

1. The insertion of the letter l in Falkirk is a misguided attempt at anglification, rightly disregarded by locals, though their present pronunciation without the 'l' probably owes more to Central Belt Scots than to considerations of etymology. The similarly named English village of Vowchurch, earlier Fowchirche (13th cent.) shows no such sign of gentrification but retains the correct form.

usually older, and with a topographical or historical reference quite separate from that of the English name. The most common examples are:

Baile Bhòid (the town of Bute)	Rothesay
Baile Dhubhthaich (the town of St Duthus)	Tain
Am Blàr Dubh (the dark field)	Muir of Ord
Bun Ilidh (the mouth of the River Ilidh)	Helmsdale
A' Chananaich (the canon, canonry)	Fortrose
A' Chomraich (the sanctuary)	Applecross
Ceann Loch Chille Chiarain (the head of the loch of St Kieran's church)	Campbeltown
Cille Chuimein (St Cumine's church)	Fort Augustus
Cill Rìmhinn (church of the king's hill)	St Andrews
An Gearasdan (the garrison)	Fort William
Inbhir Pheofharain (the mouth of the River Peffery)	Dingwall
Dùn Èideann (fort on the hill slope)	Edinburgh
A' Mhanachainn (the monastery)	Beauly
(Port) **Sgioba** (ship port)	Port Charlotte

Also some counties:

Cataibh (land of the wild-cat people)	Sutherland
Gallaibh (land of the foreigners)	Caithness

The flexibility of place names in earlier times is well illustrated by the fact that Caithness and **Cataibh** have the same root, although today they refer to different counties.

It is significant that most names of this type are on the mainland, which reflects the penetration of the English language. In fact, most Gaelic speakers from the Hebrides generally use the English form of these mainland names; the main exceptions to this are **Dùn Èideann** and **An Gearasdan**.

One of the happier features of place-names (which can sometimes be a minefield) is the frequency with which the same word occurs. In England, for instance, the multitude of places containing the word Chester/ Caster/ Caister give some idea of their background – that they were the site of a Roman camp – even if the meaning of the rest of the word is not immediately apparent. A Scottish equivalent would be **dùn,** indicating the site of an Iron-Age fort.

So, in general, the commonest roots for Gaelic place names are:

inbhir	= mouth of a river	e.g. Inverness
ceann	= head	e.g. Kinlochleven
rubha	= promontory	e.g. Rhu
creag	= rock	e.g. Craignure
baile	= township	e.g. Ballygrant
srath	= valley	e.g. Strathpeffer
caol	= strait	e.g. Kyle
druim	= ridge	e.g. Drumnadrochit
cill	= cell, church	e.g. Kilmun
dùn	= fort	e.g. Dunblane
taigh	= house	e.g. Tighnabruaich
achadh	= field	e.g. Achiltibuie

In the Hebrides and North West Highlands many of the place names are of Scandinavian origin, reflecting the period of Viking rule there (beginning c. 800 AD) The most common roots here are **sta*dh*ir**, 'farm' (which generally appears as 'sta'), hence Tolastadh (Tolsta), Scarastadh (Scarista), Lusta, etc;

setr, or **sætr**, 'dwelling', 'sheiling' (which generally appears as 'shader'), hence Grimiseadar (Grimshader), Driniseadar (Drinishader), Uigseadar (Uigshader), etc; and **bolsta***dh***r**, 'small farm' (which appears as 'bost' in e.g. Lewis and as 'bus' in Islay), hence Siabost (Shawbost), Liùrbost (Leurbost), Carabost (Carbost), etc, and Cionnabus (Kinnabus) etc.

VOCABULARY

GAELIC	ENGLISH	ENGLISH COGNATE
àireamh	number	rhyme
abhainn	river	Avon
balla	wall	bailey
coire	kettle, cauldron	corrie
còrd	agree	ac*cord*
cruinn	round	crown
cùl	back	*cul de sac* (French)
dearg	red	dark
fàsach	desert	*vast*ness
leagh	melt	leak
lighiche	doctor	leech
maor	crown officer	mayor
meud	size	metre
minig	often	many

IN THE 1930s Miss Elaine Swanson, director of the New York Language Research Institute, suggested that a basic vocabulary of no more than three hundred words was all a foreign tourist needed to 'get along' in English. To prove this she confined herself to no more than three hundred words for three months; she also suggested that this basic list applied to any language, and translated it into French, German and Italian.

Here then is Miss Swanson's list of (rather less than) three hundred words, with their equivalents in Gaelic. In the case of Gaelic (and, indeed, in other languages) there are of course instances where there is no simple equivalent, e.g. for the English 'yes' and 'no'; again, one Gaelic word will sometimes do for two English words, e.g. 'do' and 'make' (both **dèan**), or 'think' and 'thought' (both **smaoinich**). Other difficulties are noted in footnotes.

There is usually, of course, more than one Gaelic word which comes to mind as a possible translation, and so the following equivalents are, to that extent, subjective.

PREPOSITIONS

at – **aig**
after – **an dèidh**
for – **airson**
from – **bho**
in – **ann**
on – **air**
to – **do**
with – **le**

CONJUNCTIONS

and – **agus**
but – **ach**
if – **ma**
or – **no**
so – **mar sin**
that – **gu**

PRONOUNS

I – **mi**
he – **e**
me – **mi**
my – **mo**
she – **i**
their – **an**
you – **thu** (s), **sibh** (pl.)[1]
your – **do** (s), **bhur** (pl)

INTERJECTIONS

goodbye – **slàn le**
hello – **halò**
oh! – **o!**

ARTICLES

the – **am**, **an**, **a'**, **an t-**, **na**, **nan** or **nam** (depending on gender, number and case)

NATURE

fire – **teine**
light – **solas**
sun – **grian**

---

1. The traditional use of **sibh** in addressing an individual, to indicate respect, age, etc continues, but this rigidity is being questioned (as elsewhere in Europe) as society becomes less formal.

BUSINESS

bank – **banca**
pound – **not**
penny – **sgillinn**
money – **airgead**
office – **oifis**
manager – **fear-riaghlaidh**
show – **sealladh**
size – **meud**
shop – **bùth**
trouble – **dragh**
way – **slighe**

TRAVEL

boat – **bàta**
car – **càr**
country – **dùthaich**
hotel – **taigh-òsda**
left – **clì**
place – **àite**
right – **deas**
station – **stèisean**
street – **sràid**
ticket – **tiocaid**
town – **baile**
train – **trèana**

OBJECTS

bag – **màileid**
book – **leabhar**
letter – **litir**
telephone – **fòn**
thing – **rud**
story – **sgeul**
word – **facal**
picture – **dealbh**
nothing – **neoni**

DAYS OF THE WEEK

Monday – **Diluain**
Tuesday – **Dimàirt**
Wednesday – **Diciadain**
Thursday – **Diardaoin**
Friday – **Dihaoine**
Saturday – **Disathairne**
Sunday – **Didòmhnaich**

MODIFIERS

again – **a-rithist**
all – **uile**
any – **sam bith**
big – **mòr**
clean – **glan**
cold – **fuar**
dear (expensive) – **daor**
down – **sìos**
easy – **furasda**
every – **gach**
good – **math**
happy – **sona**
here – **an seo**
how? – **ciamar?**
little – **beag**
long – **fada**
many – **mòran**
more – **tuilleadh**
married – **pòsda**
much – **mòran**
new – **ùr**
nice – **gasda**
no – (make the verb negative)
not – **cha**
now – **an-dràsda**
old – **sean**
other – **eile**
piece – **pìos**
ready – **deiseil**

right (correct) – **ceart**
same – **ceudna**
slow – **mall**
some – **cuid**
sorry – **duilich**
that – **sin**
there – **an sin**
this – **seo**
too (excessive) – **ro**
also – **cuideachd**
up – **suas**
warm – **blàth**
very – **glè**
well – **gu math**
what? – **dè?**
when? – **cuin?**
where? – **càite?**
who? – **cò?**
why? – **carson?**

FOOD

bread – **aran**
butter – **ìm**
sweets – **suiteis**
coffee – **cofaidh**
egg – **ugh**
fruit – **meas**
meat – **feòil**
milk – **bainne**
salt – **salainn**
sugar – **siùcar**
vegetables – **glasraich**
water – **uisge**

TIME

day – **latha**
evening – **feasgar**
hour – **uair**
minute – **mionaid**

month – **mìos**
morning – **madainn**
night – **oidhche**
time – **ùine**
today – **an-diugh**
tonight – **a-nochd**
tomorrow – **a-màireach**
week – **seachdain**
yesterday – **an-dè**

HOUSE

bath – **bath**[2]
floor – **làr**
house – **taigh**
key – **iuchair**
room – **seòmar**
table – **bòrd**

PEOPLE

boy – **balach**
brother – **bràthair**
doctor – **dotair**
father – **athair**
friend – **caraid**
girl – **caileag**
man – **duine**
men – **daoine**
miss – **maighdeann**
mother – **màthair**
Mr – **maighstir**
Mrs – **bean-phòsda**
name – **ainm**
one – **aon**
policeman – **poileas**
sister – **piuthar**
woman – **boireannach**
women – **boireannaich**

---

2. Most Gaelic speakers simply use the English word.

CLOTHES

cloth – **clò**
clothes – **aodach**
coat – **còta**
dress – **dreasa**
hat – **ad**
shoes – **brògan**
stockings – **stocainnean**
trousers – **briogais**

COLOUR

black – **dubh**
blue – **gorm**
green – **uaine**
red – **dearg**
white – **geal**

VERBS

to. . .[3]
will – **-(a)idh**
won't – **cha**
ask – **faighnich**
be – **bi**
am – **tha**
are – **tha**
is – **tha**
was – **bha**
were – **bha**
can – **is urrainn**
can't – **chan urrainn**
could – **b'urrainn**
come – **thig**
came – **thàinig**
do – **dèan**
did – **rinn**
does – **tha (e) a' dèanamh**
don't (imperative) – **na**

---

3. For the infinitive see chapter 6.

eat – **ith**
ate – **dh'ith**
excuse – **gabh leisgeul**
get – **faigh**
got – **fhuair**
give – **thoir**
go – **rach**
went – **chaidh**
have – **tha aig**
has – **tha aig**
had – **bha aig**
have to – **feumaidh**
help – **cuidich**
know – **tha fios aig**
knew – **bha fios aig**
learn – **ionnsaich**
like – **is toigh le**
make – **dèan**
made – **rinn**
must – **feumaidh**
please – **toilich**
put – **cuir**
gain – **buannaich**
read – **leugh**
say – **abair**
said – **thubhairt**
see – **faic**
saw – **chunnaic**
sent – **chuir**
sit – **suidh**
sat – **shuidh**
sleep – **caidil**
slept – **chaidil**
smoke – **smoc**
start (begin) – **tòisich**
stop – **stad**
take – **gabh**
took – **ghabh**
thank – **thoir taing**

think – **smaoinich**
thought – **smaoinich**
understand – **tuig**
understood – **thuig**
use – **cuir gu feum**
want – **iarr**
work – **obraich**
write – **sgrìobh**
wrote – **sgrìobh**

VOCABULARY

GAELIC	ENGLISH	ENGLISH COGNATE
amadan	fool	un-minded
balg	bag	bulge
bràghad	neck, throat	*bronch*ial
bruich	boil, cook	brew, broth
caraid	friend	charity
connadh	fuel	candle
crùb	crouch	creep
cuileag	a fly	culex, *culic*iform
dàil	delay	dwell
duilich	sorry	dolour
fios	knowledge	*vis*ion
leugh	read	*leg*ible
màl	rent, payment	black*mail*
meall	deceive	*mal*treat, *mal*ice
miann	desire	mean

Some place names derived from words mentioned in this chapter.

Teine – Fire
Ardentinny (Cowal)

Baile – Town
Ballachulish (Glencoe)

Dubh – Black
Cairndow (Cowal)
Douglas (Lanarkshire)

Gorm – Green, Blue
Cairngorm

Uaine – Green
Arduaine (Argyll)

Dearg – Red
Beinn Dearg (Ross and Cromarty)

Geal – White
Gelder (Aberdeenshire)

Suidhe – Seat
Amhuinnsuidhe (Harris)